I'm Reading About

MARYLAND

The Old Line State!

GALLOPADE

by Carole Marsh

Printed and Manufactured in Peachtree City, GA., USA
www.gallopade.com

Book design: John Hanson

Editorial manager: Janice Baker

Maryland is a great state.

It is one of a kind.

What makes Maryland special?

Let's read about it

and see!

NATIVE AMERICANS

Who lived in Maryland first?

Native Americans did!

They moved around to find food.
They hunted in Maryland's woods.
They fished in Maryland's rivers.
They gathered fruits and seeds and nuts.

EXPLORERS

The first explorers came to Maryland in 1524.
They came from the country of France.

Giovanni da Verrazzano was their leader.
He and his men were looking for new land!

SETTLEMENT

Settlers from England arrived in Maryland in 1634.
They traveled on two ships called
the *Ark* and the *Dove*.
They named their settlement St. Mary's.

Maryland was one of
the original 13 colonies.

St. Mary's

STATEHOOD

Maryland was the seventh state
to join the United States of America!

Isn't it great,
to be a state!
I bet Maryland
could hardly wait!

Maryland became a state in 1788.

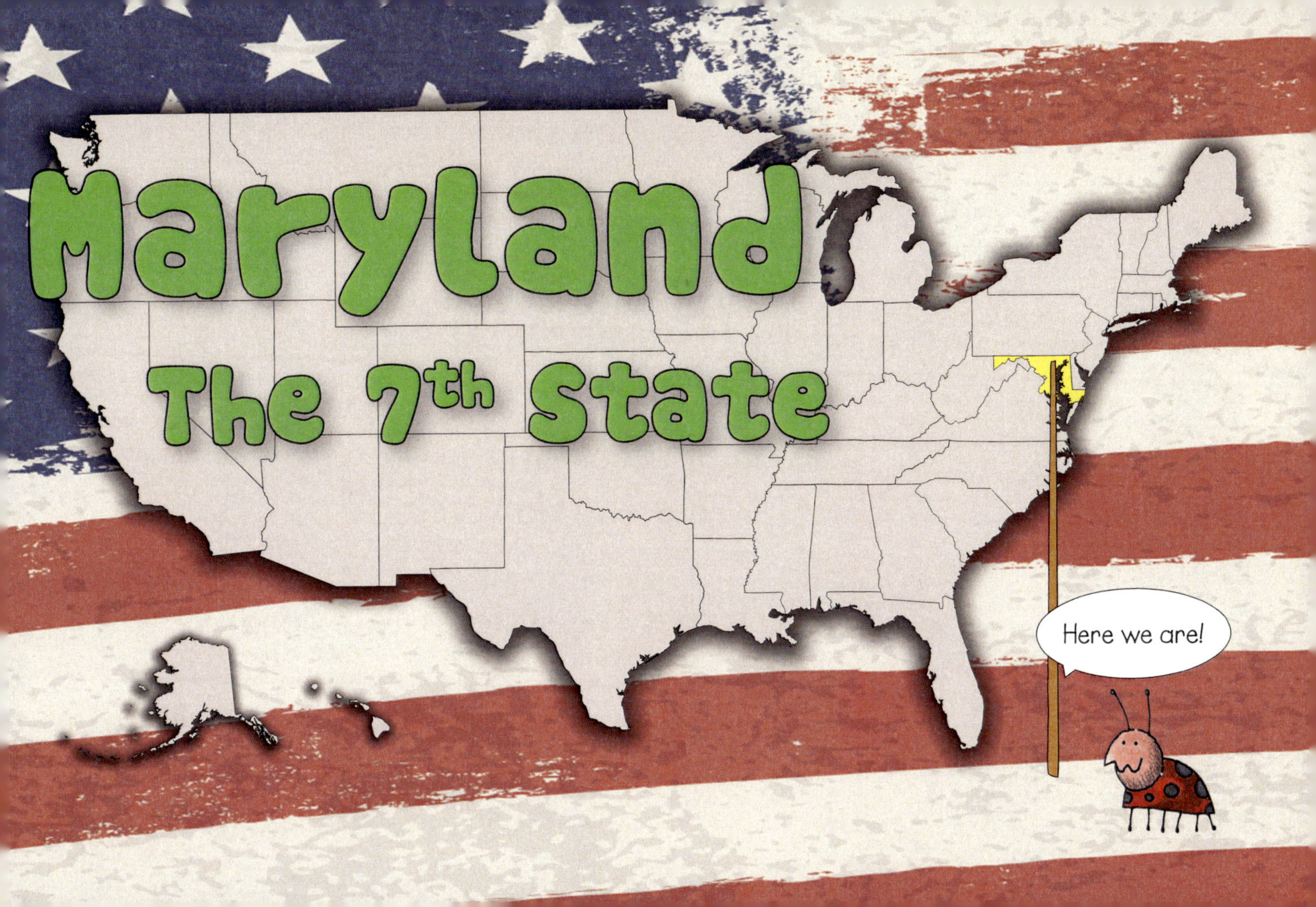
Maryland
The 7th State
Here we are!

FLAG

I am the state flag.
I was adopted in 1904.

What colors am I?
Red. White. Black. Gold.

Look at me.
What else do you see?

I fly high over the state of Maryland!

CAPITAL

Say hello to Annapolis,
the capital city of Maryland!

There is an important building in Annapolis.
It is the State House.
Maryland's laws are made there!

State House

SEAL

I am a seal,
but I am not the State Seal.
If I were, I would be very important.
I would be stamped on many official papers.
(Ouch, that might hurt!)

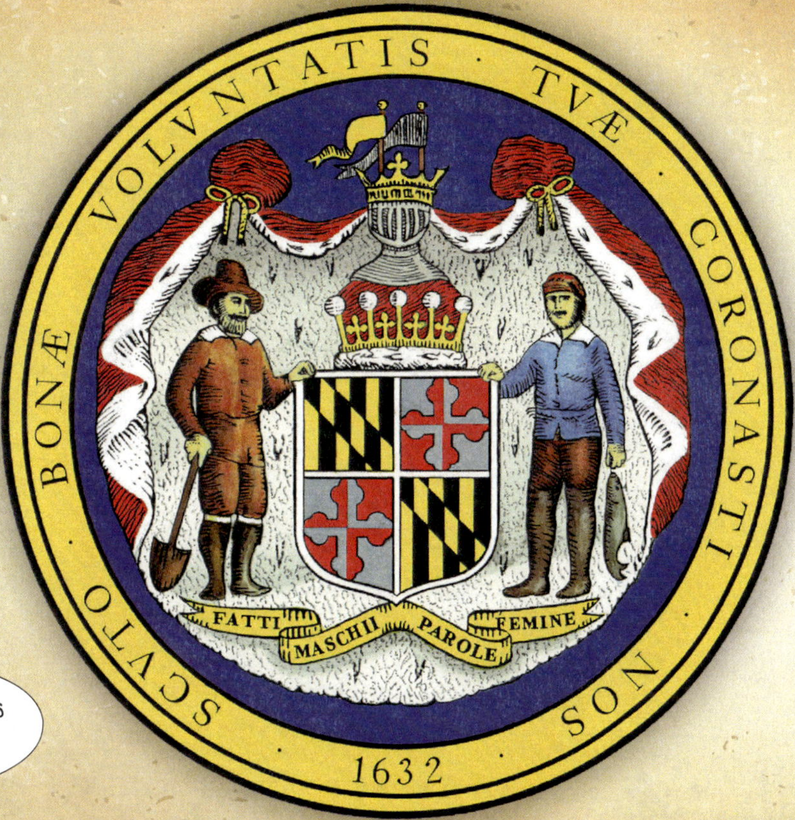
SCVTO · BONÆ VOLVNTATIS · TVÆ · CORONASTI · NOS
1632
FATTI MASCHII PAROLE FEMINE

Now, that's official!

NICKNAME

State nicknames are fun!
State nicknames are great!
They share fun facts
about each state!

Maryland nickname is "The Old Line State."

Maryland has other nicknames.
They include the "Free State" and
"America in Miniature."

The Old Line State

BORDERS

Look at Maryland.
Maryland is in a region called "the Mid-Atlantic."

Maryland borders four other states.
It also borders Washington, D.C.

Find Maryland's neighbors on the map!

Borders

PENNSYLVANIA
WASHINGTON D.C.
DELAWARE
MARYLAND
WEST VIRGINIA
VIRGINIA
CHESAPEAKE BAY
ATLANTIC OCEAN
Howdy, neighbors!

COUNTIES

Maryland is divided into 24 counties.
Counties are a form of local government.
Counties provide services that people need!
Those services include:

Schools **Parks** **Libraries** **Police**

Firefighters **and More!**

Counties

MARYLAND'S CAPITAL, ANNAPOLIS, IS IN ANNE ARUNDEL COUNTY.

PEOPLE

Many famous people

Francis Scott Key

Wrote the lyrics to "The Star Spangled Banner," the U.S. national anthem

Frederick Douglass

Escaped slave who became a world-famous abolitionist

Harriett Tubman

Escaped slave who led other slaves to freedom on the Underground Railroad

call our state home!

PEOPLE

Babe Ruth

Major league baseball player who set many hitting records

Thurgood Marshall

First African American U.S. Supreme Court Justice

Jim Henson

Creator of the Muppets that appear on the *Sesame Street* television show

Baltimore Oriole

BIRD

I am the state bird, and I fly
over Maryland, proud and high.

As I fly, up in the sky,
I flap my wings to tell you "Hi!"

The Maryland state bird is the Baltimore Oriole.

Black-eyed Susan

FLOWER

I am the Black-eyed Susan.
I am the state flower.

I grow where it's warm and sunny.
I bloom in spring and summer.
I help make Maryland beautiful!

Look at me! Smell me!
I am part of the sunflower family
of flowers.

White Oak

TREE

I am a White Oak—I'm the state tree.
All over Maryland is where to find me.

My roots run deep, they keep me strong.
I can live for hundreds of years—that's very long!

I stand up straight, big and tall.
Don't climb too high—it would hurt to fall!

Baltimore Checkerspot Butterfly

I am the Baltimore Checkerspot Butterfly.
I am the state insect.

I flit and I fly from flower to flower.
I am looking for nectar to drink.

Look at my beautiful wings.
What colors do you see?

INSECT

Chesapeake Bay
Let's go boating!

Let's go to Chesapeake Bay!

We can swim in the waves.
We can ride on a boat.

We can fish in the water,
or relax on a float.

Maryland's Chesapeake Bay is home to many animals:

Fish **Oysters** **Birds** **Crabs** **Eels** **and More!**

CHESAPEAKE BAY

Mountains

MOUNTAINS

Maryland's mountains are the place to be.
Hiking, fishing, camping—
fun for you and me.

Winter weather brings lots of snow.
Temperatures drop to freezing and below!

Rivers

RIVERS

Maryland has many rivers.
People like to use rivers for boating and fishing!

This habitat is home to many animals:

Birds Deer Snakes Frogs Fish and More!

The Patuxent River is the longest river in Maryland!

Fort McHenry

LANDMARK

Fort McHenry is located at the entrance to the Port of Baltimore.
It is a military fort shaped like a star.

The fort is well known for its role during the War of 1812.
A battle there kept the British from taking over Baltimore Harbor!

Francis Scott Key wrote the U.S. national anthem about the Battle of Fort McHenry.
He wrote it while the fort was under attack!

Maryland Crops

AGRICULTURE

Maryland has many farms.
Why?
Because Maryland has good soil and a mild climate!

Some of Maryland's top crops are:

Corn **Soybeans** **Nursery Products** **Apples**

Sports in Maryland

SPORTS

Baseball! Basketball! Football!
Maryland has it all.

Whether you like to watch or play,
You are sure to have a ball!

Orioles **Ravens** **Terrapins**

Midshipmen

& More!

Maryland: Home of Blue Crabs

CLAIM TO FAME

Maryland is famous for its delicious blue crabs! People enjoy steamed crab and tasty crab cakes. Crabmeat is also used in soups, dips, and many other recipes.

Male blue crabs have blue tips on their front claws. The male crabs have more meat than the female ones.

GLOSSARY

abolitionist: someone who worked to end slavery in the U.S.

climate: weather conditions in an area over a long period of time

colony: a settlement ruled by another country

habitat: a place where plants or animals naturally live

laws: rules made by the government

lyrics: the words of a song

national anthem: a country's official song

nectar: a sweet liquid produced by plants, especially flowers

region: an area that has similar characteristics

settlement: the first community in an area